Be cheerful

This book belongs to

Written by Stephen Barnett
Illustrated by Rosie Brooks

Contents

About this book

Using short paragraphs comprising of lucid sentences, this book encourages young readers to read, understand and enjoy stories based on themes that they can easily relate to.

Be cheerful

We cannot be happy all the time. All of us feel a little sad or worried sometimes.

Sometimes we are worried about
something that might happen to
us or to our family and friends.

Many a time we feel sad
because we miss someone who
is far away from us.

Sometimes we are afraid of
something. It maybe an animal
or a person.

Often we feel like this because
we are lonely or tired.

Most of the things we worry
about do not happen!

We can be cheerful again by
thinking about happy things...

...or by doing something nice like
baking a cake!

Did you know that when we are
happy and cheerful, we make
others happy too!

Do your best

I was working hard on a project.
It was my homework. The project
was on birds and animals.

I was worried that my project was not good enough. I felt that it could be made better.

My father watched while I was drawing some birds. He liked my drawing.

But I was not sure. I thought that everyone else would have much better projects than mine!

My father smiled and said that all my friends would also be worried about their projects just like me!

My father wanted to know if I had done my best while making the project.

I told him that I had done my
best. He said that is all what
anybody could do.

Your family is like a treasure

We all live in families. Families come in all sizes.

Some people come from small families while some belong to really large ones.

Some families have
grandparents and lots of uncles,
aunts and cousins.

Other families are smaller with just one parent and a child. They stay alone.

Sometimes some people might live far away. They do not meet their family for a long time.

Other families live together and
see each other everyday.

Families are like a treasure. Your family is always there for you when you need them.

Your family will listen to you when you have a problem. They will cheer you up when you are sad.

Always look after your family. A
family is like a treasure that is
more valuable than gold!

New words

cheerful

happy

always

sometimes

worried

family

friends

happen

miss

afraid

lonely

tired

worry

happen

nice

baking

working

project

homework

enough

watched

better

anybody

size

large

grandparents

cousins

smaller

live

everyday

treasure

close

family

listen

cheer

sad

problem

valuable

What did you learn?

Be cheerful
What colour are the girl's gumboots?
What is the colour of the pillow on the girl's bed?
What is the girl doing in the kitchen?

Do your best
What was the boy's project about?
What was he drawing?
What did the boy answer to his father's questions?

Your family is like a treasure
What colour is the telephone?
How can your family help you when you have a problem?